Email Marketing 2018

Email Marketing Secrets Bundle

New, Simple and Effective Email Marketing Tips and Tricks to Revamp Your Business, Get More Customers and Generate More Sales

By

James Ford

Copyright notice

Copyright © 2018

CONTENTS

James Ford

INTRODUCTION

Irvine CA, 5 Years Ago...

So I was trying to get a job as a waiter.

I had a stable job. I was supporting my family. But I felt like something was missing. Not only did I loathe my job, but we had another kid on the way.

So even with a professional background, a professional degree, and a professional job, I figured I'd start waiting tables so I could make some extra dough on the side (logical, right?).

And little did I know, trying to get a job waiting tables was one of the hardest things I ever had to do!

Why Was This So Hard?

I kept getting rejection after rejection-- yes, from restaurants and bars!-- because I didn't have what it took to "wait tables". Seriously?!

You can imagine how this felt. Was I really not good enough to even wait one lousy table?

Bruised ego aside, I still held on to my dream of making a little more money so that I could enjoy spending more time with my family, supporting them, and actually doing work that I enjoyed.

So because restaurants were throwing my resume out the window, this was the exact point in my life I started blogging online.

And I happened to get introduced to email marketing.

Now, I'm a "fast learner" kind of guy or so I thought.

So even though I had heard that email marketing wasn't all the beds and roses it was supposed to be, I knew I could overcome the "steep learning curve" and "mind boggling" issues I'd heard so many people dealing with.

It couldn't be that hard, right?

I had never been more wrong in my life

What was this alien force that hijacked my will to continue and left me feeling like I might as well quit while I'm ahead?

I went from a self-proclaimed "fast learner guy" to feeling dumb, frustrated, and even "crazy" because I couldn't for the life of me figure out how this darn email marketing thing worked!

What Did I Do?

How did I solve the mind boggling problem?

I put my nose down and invested all of my energy into figuring the thing out.

All those thousands of hours I could have been blogging on, I spent on reading every email marketing and list building book,

...watching every tutorial,

...reading every comment,

...in every forum,

To see if I could find people like me...people who understood what I was going through!

I'm sure you've felt like this before, but when you're deep in the process of something, you feel like you'll never get out of it.

And I did think of all the other things I could have been doing with my time instead of trying to master email marketing...which I did end up eventually doing.

Hi, I'm James. I have about 40,000 people on my list... And while impressive, I know tons of gurus in our niche alone who have lists much bigger than that.

However, few of them bank $17,000 for over the course of a 3-day product launch, like I do... ALL THE TIME whenever I launch any of my courses!

I'm going to assume that traffic may be part of your problem, and that is what's stopping you.

If that's the case - you're doing it wrong.

It's one of those Chicken vs. Egg things. Do you wait until you get the traffic before you start building the email list or do you know what you're going to say to that list before you build?

I'd contend that if you have the message in place first... It's psychologically a million times easier to then build that email list.

That's why I've written...

"Email Marketing Secrets Bundle: New, Simple and Effective Email Marketing Tips and Tricks to Revamp Your Business, Get More Customers and Generate More Sales"

What's Inside?

1. 2018 Tips on How to Get New Customers

2. How to Generate More Sales

3. How to Build Trust and Authority

Why this guide was originally never slotted to see the light of day, it started out as a private mentoring session with one of my private coaching clients.

In fact, it wasn't even meant to go out in public. But once we got going... I just couldn't stop.

I didn't hold back at all.

I spilled my guts and left no stone unturned. And that's why, when it was all done... I decided to release it.

And that's because I wanted to give you all the stuff that matters when it comes to email marketing...

Excited yet?

Without wasting any more time, let's

get started.

James Ford

CHAPTER 1

HOW TO GET NEW CUSTOMERS

Imagine this scenario,

You want to buy a new computer...

You are getting tired of the one you are

using.

Step one: You go window shopping

online. You check out the different

brands with the different

specifications. Hell, you even browse through forums and ask questions. But you do not want to pony up any cash. Not yet anyways.

Step two: Day after day, the performance of your computer keeps getting worse - shuts at intervals and without notice. You try to console yourself that it is still not time to get a new one. But you go through another round of window shopping. Only this time, you narrow down your options based on your previous experience.

At last, when you can no longer bear the trauma your computer is putting you through; you go ahead and buy a new one.

The truth is you are *not* the only one who goes through this kind of "buying cycle." Many others - even clients who eventually order for your service or product - do the same.

They become more serious or "more needy" for your service or product when the current service provider is no longer adequate for them.

The real secret is to catch when they are ready to bite the bullet and order for a better service (let's use providing a service as our case study).

The problem now is ... How will you know when they are ready to order for a better service without being a mind reader of sorts?

The answer? Email marketing!

It is important that you realize that the people who land on your website or any other website are still going through a "window shopping" phase at that time when they land on your website.

Some who still even go to the extent of making enquiries either through the contact form on your website or via phone are still "window shopping".

The best way to stay on top of their minds is to ask for their contact, notably, their email addresses.

And when you ask for their email address, it is only wise if you send them cool emails on a regular basis.

Thus, when they are finally ready to buy, you would be their first choice.

This works provided you do it right.

And the not-that fun fact is, they came to you without having the intention of buying from you (since they were actually window shopping; just in case you have forgotten).

If I had to narrow it down to the top three steps you should take to step up your email marketing game, they would be....

Step One:

Give Them a Compelling Reason to Give You Their Email Address

Here is an example, when you decide to sign up on Spotify; they will give you the opportunity of signing up for the premium plan (which does not have any ads) for 7 days free of charge.

Before the expiration of your 7 days free trial, you will receive another email to sign up for a 30 day trial (although you are given 14 days to make a decision to sign up for the 30 day trial).

See the image below;

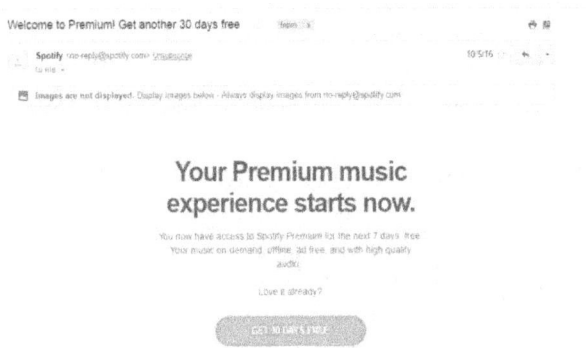

The rationale behind this is simple: if you sign up, especially for the 30 days free trial, you are more inclined to pay for the premium plan.

This is easy to get started with, especially if you loathe content creation. And let's face it; you will still need to constantly update your content from time to time.

But with a discount offering, the work is done just once.

I like, scratch that, I love this opt in offer more than content most of which are even rehashed anyways.

However, before you call the content

dogs on me, you can...

**Give away solid content as your opt in
offer**

This is pretty much the industry

standard.

You give away either one of your low

priced products or any useful and

actionable content that solves a specific

problem for your niche market in exchange for an email address.

For example, go through the bullet points of any paid product. Extract two or three of the bullet points, research and write on these. Then, give the report away.

Checklist

Here's a simple 3-step checklist that your content must pass through;

- Solve a problem related to your services

- The solution must also be related

- Your content must be *useful* - not fluff.

Re-read that last sentence multiple times until it makes sense to you.

Done, right?

Let's continue.

I asked you to perform that little exercise because this content is your best chance to show how much of an 'expert' you or your brand is.

If your content is full of information that can be found on the first page of Google, then, obviously, you have shot yourself in the foot.

Checklist number one above must never be ignored if you want to have the right persons on your list.

Quality over quantity, my friend!

Your content should cause those that sign up to have "sleepless nights" until they buy one of your products.

You know I meant by "sleepless nights" literally, right?

Well, just saying.

A variation of content as an opt in offer

If you have been following our discussion, I told you earlier that you can give away one of your low priced product as your opt in offer.

A variation of this is to offer one of your medium priced products (usually

$40 - $150) as a bonus to someone

who is having a product launch.

Notes:

1. You can also do this if you have a

   software-as-a-service   (saas)

   business.

2. What you are giving as a bonus

   should be related in some way to

the product launch. Think yoga and nutrition, list building and email marketing (duh!)

When you do this, you have a buyers list and not just prospects (you better treat them well).

In order to get your list of subscribers, those that sign up to receive your bonus can be sent to you in XLS or you design a special squeeze page for them.

See the image below for an example;

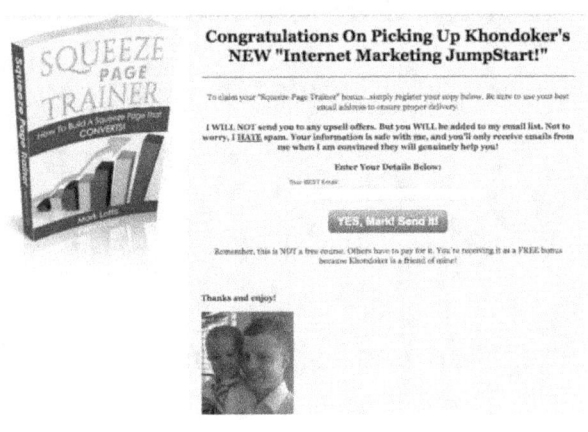

Yes, this method works in just about

any niche. Thanks for asking.

Step Two:

Provide More than One Way for

Sign Up

Can you pretend that you want to do some window shopping for a list building tool?

If you can, I will give a resource which shows a full detail of how to place opt in forms in almost every page of your website.

Here is the link to the resource; it is a 45-paged monster review.

Yes, on that page, Robbie reviewed thrive themes. But take your eyes off the promotion for the tool.

Instead, discover a full illustration of placing your opt in forms on multiple pages. If you are technophobic or it takes you a while to figure out tech stuffs, start using thrive right away.

You can use your analytics to test and tweak your options in order to get the best results.

Infusionsoft, Convertkit, Drip, Aweber, Getresponse Or Mailchimp? *Which One Should You Choose?*

Mailchimp if you starting out on a shoestring budget. Mailchimp is forever free for your first 2,000 subscribers. Convertkit if you have a little money to spend.

It is $29 for the first 1,000 subscribers.

Why Convertkit?

Two words - better automation.

Convertkit is just like Infusionsoft, but it is easier to use than Infusionsoft.

Side notes;

1. If you do not want to mess around with tags, and all that geeky stuff, stick with Mailchimp.

2. You can get Convertkit for free for the first 30 days. Sshh? Don't tell anyone.

Here's how...

From time to time, Nathan Barry (the founder of Convertkit) or any member of his team partners with other persons with good email lists to provide webinar training mostly on automation.

On this webinar and after the webinar, you are offered a 30day free trial on Convertkit.

The list owners that have partnered with Convertkit like this include Joseph Michael, Amy Porterfield, David Siteman Garland, and Bryan Harris. Just to mention a few.

Now here is the main secret, most of the times the webinar replays are available for as long as 21 days.

So, if you search for recent webinars from Convertkit, chances are you can easily snag a 30-day free trial on Convertkit.

Step Three:

Build Authority And Keep Doing So.

This will be discussed in the last outline of this guide.

Step Four:

Involve Your Audience

The best way for you to do this is to ask questions.

Ask open-ended questions - questions that easily strike up a conversation.

Two examples of questions you can ask are;

"Suggest one thing you would like to see in our product/service that is not currently there?"

"Which part of the product do you find difficult to implement?"

Asking questions provides you a means

of;

- Growing closer to your audience

- Gaining a deeper understanding

    of their interests

- Getting your subscribers to take action and

- Engaging your audience. This result in more open rates and more sales on the long term.

Step Five:

Make Use of Forums

Put a strong call to action in your forum signature.

If you continue to get involved in specific and targeted forum activities, you will easily get subscribers.

How successful this method is depends on:

1. How involved you are in forum activities.

2. You answering questions related to what's on your signature.

On a final note, see unsubscribes as a good thing.

Here are my top two reasons;

- They are no longer interested in your message for whatever reason. Fine, let them go, otherwise, they will be hurting

analytics.

- You do not have to pay for what

   you do not use. If you have lots of

   those who are not interested in

   your message, you will still be

   paying for those subscribers.

   Since you pay based on the

   number of subscribers you have.

The best thing about email marketing is that it opens up at least two avenues for you to make sales.

1. Those who are ready to make a purchase now

2. Those who will be ready to make a purchase at some other time in the future.

With a combination of list building and

email marketing, you can have fun and

still grow your business. Let's discuss...

James Ford

CHAPTER 2

HOW TO GENERATE MORE SALES

One of the true beauties of email marketing is automation.

These set of messages are called "autoresponder messages."

You can create a set of messages which new subscribers receive for as long as you still have an account with the email service provider.

If you are still struggling with more traffic and consequently more sales when using your autoresponder after trying a handful of strategies, the six additional strategies shared in this chapter will be of help.

1. Allow Your Buyers Sell Your Products

So recently, I bought Graphic Dashboard by Robert Plank.

In the members' area, there is a link for me to sell this product and keep 100% of the sales made.

Now, you can also do something similar, even if the product is not a software like Graphic Dashboard.

As you must have noticed, I mentioned buyers, that is, not everybody on your list. Are you following at all?

Why buyers?

Buyers have experienced the product; they are more likely to sell with honesty because it is based on their experience.

But don't try this if your product is crap. Well, you can, but be prepared for loads of refunds.

Here is a sample email of what you can send to your buyers;

Subject line: how does [$x] per sale sound to you?

Hi *[first name]*,

My name is [your name], and I run the affiliate program over at [link]. The reason I'm writing today is to offer you the chance to join our affiliate team – and to make this deal extra sweet, I'm going to throw in some perks that aren't available to the general affiliates.

Take a look:

[$x] per sale on the frontend – that's a special commission rate of [x%], and as you can see those sales will add up fast.

[x%] commission rates on the backend.

Great conversions – right now the sales letter is converting at [x%], and [y%] of customers are grabbing the backend deal too.

Special bonus for your customers - Your customers will love getting [name of bonus] for free, and you'll love the bump to your conversion rate.

Personalized landing page - You can see yours here: [link]

Full set of swipes and creatives to make promoting this offer easier than ever!

Looks good, right?

Now you're probably wondering if this product will appeal to your customers. I'm absolutely certain it will, because [quick *description of product and why it will appeal to affiliate's customers].*

But you don't even need to take my word for it. Instead, please check out this review copy of the product, and see if you don't agree that your customers will love this: [link to review copy].

I think you'll agree this is a great opportunity for you to give your customers the solutions they need, while creating nice paychecks for yourself.

So your next step is easy – log into your affiliate account at [link]

I've already set you up with the following information:

Username: [insert username]

Password: [insert password]

If you have any questions let me know – I'm here to help!

[sign off]

*P.s. Still not sure? Let me sweeten the pot
again...*

*I'll bump your commission rate for the next
two weeks to [x%]. That means that any sales
you make between now and [end date in two
weeks] will put [$x] in your pocket. You'll
make more money without doing any extra
work.*

So get your affiliate link now at [link] to get started – and I look forward to personally welcoming you onboard!

And that's it!

Hell, you can even run an affiliate contest solely with your buyers.

If you decide to go through this route, here is a sample email that you can send;

Subject line: who else wants to win [some cool gift, like cash, an ipad, etc]?

Hi [name],

It's [your name] here with an exciting announcement about the [general name of affiliate program] affiliate program. You're going to love this!

Here's the scoop…

We're launching an affiliate contest on [date] with over [monetary value – e.g., dollar amount] worth of cash and prizes to be given away. This is the hottest affiliate contest of the year, so you don't want to miss this!

Here's what you could win:

[insert a table or description of the cash and prizes the top affiliates could win in the contest. For best results, include some random draw prizes where anyone who makes at least one sale is eligible to win. That way, even your smaller affiliates will promote during the contest period since they too have a shot of winning some great cash or prizes.]

Mark your calendar for [beginning date] to start promotions. The contest runs until [end date], so be sure to log into your affiliate account to grab your links, swipes and creatives: [link to affiliate center].

Good luck!

[sign your name]

P.s. Hope to see you on the contest leader board! But you have to promote to win, so get *your links now and start planning your*

winning promotional strategy!

Ok you got that. But don't go on trying

to turn your buyers to slick salesmen.

Suffice to say, you will lose your

credibility and your business will suffer

for it.

Alright, moving on,

2. Offer A Flash Sale

The best way to do this is to give prospects who are yet to make a purchase from you or who have not bought any product for some time a high discount on a premium product related to the freebie they downloaded.

Be prepared for lots of sales within a short time.

Word of caution; make sure you are offering a damn good of a deal.

Don't just slap anything together in the name of offering a deal.

That won't sound cool, trust me.

We don't want to ruin our relationship with our subscribers, right?

Well I don't, you may.

Next,

3. Offer Training Via Webinars

If you prefer adding training instead of using only mails, then, webinars are a sure way to train your subscribers.

You can offer to train a segment or all of your subscribers. The choice is yours.

Then, on the webinar you offer them a discount on your premium product as discussed in the strategy #2.

With webinars, you are indirectly creating content to send your subscribers.

Here's how...

You will send an email

- For them to register

- To remind them of the webinar and how to log in. This is usually a couple of emails spanning over a few days.

- To remind them to watch the replay. You can make this time limited, like 3 days after which the webinar (and the discount offer made on the webinar is pulled)

It is good practice to...

- Offer a workbook and/or additional material for those that registered

- Offer additional discounts or cash to those that stayed till the end of the webinar.

Unto the next tip,

4. Promote Related Offers

This is one reason why you should invest in a good email service provider.

When someone makes a purchase, you can tag them and send them follow up emails to promote related offers.

If your email service provider does not have this feature, a crude way for you to do this is to create a new squeeze page specifically for this purpose.

For example, if someone just purchased a software product, a related product can be a video training detailing how they can make money offering a service using the software.

5. Resend To Your Un-Opens

Warning; don't do this often. Otherwise, you will dilute its importance.

This is very useful during launches. That is why you should refrain from participating in every launch out there.

If you are using Aweber, the platform helps you with picking out the best times to send your emails.

But even at that, it is not possible for everybody to open your emails.

A better option is to resend the emails to those that did not open the first time.

It is possible that some actually opened it but it did not reflect on the open stats. This means that they will receive the same message twice.

It does not matter; this number will be very small so this should not deter you from sending to un-opens.

Before re-sending the emails, change the headline. Mailchimp and rip for example, allows you to write a new headline which it will send to un-opens.

So you do the job once...

You write a new headline to be sent to un-opens and

You choose the waiting period before the second email is sent.

If you are still not comfortable sending this email twice, you add the following introduction to the second email to be sent;

"I wasn't sure whether or not you got this email the first time I sent it. It's important, so I just wanted to make sure you didn't miss it. Here it is again…"

If you get some whiners, ignore them.

If you cannot stand their complaints, delete them off your list!

6. Answer Questions from Your Subscribers

This might not lead to a sale but it will surely help you

- Establish trust with your audience.

- Eliminate lack of content

For you to generate a sale from this, you will need to have a detailed course related to the question asked by your subscriber.

Here's how it works...

A subscriber asks you a question,

You answer the question ...truthfully.

But you indicate that for a complete understanding of the subject matter...

Then, you provide a link to one of your products.

You can even take this further by providing a time limited discount for the said product just because someone asked a related question.

By now you have a clear understanding of how to generate sales. If you are still in the dark, read the section again.

Still have any questions? Send me a mail.

Next up, how can you build authority?

Find out next.

CHAPTER 3

HOW TO BUILD TRUST AND AUTHORITY

Trust is one thing that you can build with toil and sweat for a number of years and destroy in seconds.

If you want to build trusted relationships with your friends and/or clients, you need to put in the time and the effort.

Let me use the following example to further illustrate my point...

There was a bike lock called kryptonite.

For a long time, people all over the world held the belief was that this bike lock is the most secure one in the entire universe.

However, one day a YouTube video went viral and in the video, a guy showed how to use a ballpoint pen tip

pick a kryptonite lock and even do so

within seconds.

This video was just one minute long,

but it destroyed a long held belief and

trust in the security of a kryptonite

bike lock.

One very important aspect of building your list is to establish trust.

I know what you are thinking;

"How can I stand out and keep standing out in the midst of the endless amounts of noise out there?"

Yea, I know that's what you are thinking because I am a mind reader of sorts.

However, do not book an appointment with me because you will be sorely disappointed.

Okay, I was saying you can effectively build trust and authority with the people on your list by making use of the following four strategies;

1. *Show Up Regularly*

Email your list with quality content and do so on a consistent basis.

Your autoresponder sequence is your best way of doing this without running almost beserk.

Simply create the messages beforehand and load them into your automated series.

You can then keep adding more with time.

Here's what I did the first time I was setting this up,

- I loaded up 21 emails at a go. (The emails were to be sent on a daily basis)

- I recorded the date.

- I continue to promote my landing page

  (in between my promotions, I created the time to write more sequences.)

- After 17 days, I loaded up the ones I just wrote and

- I kept on repeating the process until I was satisfied with the number of subscribers I had on my list.

- Then, I started sending broadcast

  messages.

Use my strategy as you deem fit - copy

it or modify it.

Think about this for a moment;

You have two friends;

One rarely talks to you, the other keeps

in touch with you on a constant basis.

When the two needs your help, which one will you be more inclined to help?

Your choice is as good as mine - the one that regularly kept in touch.

That's the way it should be with email list.

Do not just email them when you are in need of emergency cash.

2. *Add Value To The Lives Of Your Subscribers.*

From experience, three of the best ways to do this are;

- Answer their questions.

- Fulfill their aspirations

- Surprise them. Send them digital gifts. For example, a friend of mine usually asks his buyers to fill in the physical addresses after they have bought from him. He then sends physical cards to them afterwards. You can replicate this or think of something better for your audience.

Before hitting the send button (or schedule button), ask yourself..."is there anything valuable in this email?" if you can answer with a resounding yes, then, hit the send button.

3. *"Borrow" Authority*

If you are short of the content that you

can provide for your audience, then,

this becomes your "go to" method.

Simply find a worthy resource related

to your market and more important

has the kind of value you want to pass

across. This resource can be news

websites (eg. New York Times, or Wall

Street Journal), YouTube or a blog post that you found useful for yourself.

Chances are that if the blog post adds value to you, it can do the same for your subscribers.Here's an example of how to do this;

Let's say you are searching for a cool article on email marketing open rates.

A quick search on Google like this one

➔

"Site:nytimes.com   open   rates   email

marketing"

...will return relevant articles written

by the New York Times on this subject.

In fact, let's do this together.

Here's what Google returned...

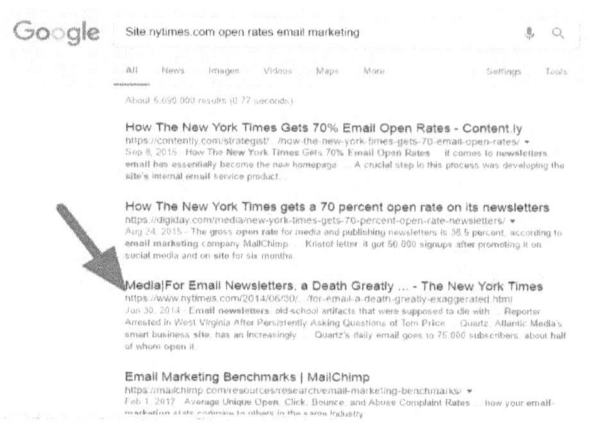

This method can work for any other trustworthy news source.

Here are more examples you can try out:

Site:wsj.com keyword

Site:techcrunch.com keyword

Site:[yourfavoritenewssite.com] keyword

Here is an example of a subject line you can use;

Subject: *[news source] loves/hates [topic]*

Here is an example of a body copy that you can use;

Did you know that according to the New York Times, a high open rate in email marketing does not lead to more sales?

Though, with this method, you cannot add your call to action within the content of the email, you can add it in the PS of your email.

You are wrong.

Yes, you are because you think citing other experts' shows that you are not that knowledgeable about your field.

You cannot be more "wronger"...lol

You accomplish two things when you reference other experts in your niche/market;

- You ride on the authority of this expert resource

- You further lend credence to your commitment of providing the best value to your subscribers.

- You get to receive "thank you" messages from your subscribers for letting them know that this kind of content exists.

- You are assured of future dividends as a result of your benevolence.

4. *Admit that you are human*

If you have made a mistake, own up to it.

Do not fake it though.

It only shows that you are human and not a superman.

"Apologize for sending out the wrong deal, an inaccurate fact, or a broken link. It's an opportunity to build trust,"

says <u>Wendy Burtthomas</u>.

"Admit your mistake and explain how you'll correct the problem in the future."

"Consumers recognize that companies make mistakes," adds <u>Loren Mcdonald</u> at Silverpop.

"In fact, acknowledging and properly acting on an error can often result in a more engaged customer."

With time, you can build trust and authority with these strategies.

Let's conclude.

James Ford

FINAL NOTES

There is a process involved before you become a success with anything in life.

The same is true with email marketing.

Two effective ways of improving your email marketing campaigns is to;

- Plan well

- Keep testing and tweaking based on your data

You can only test and tweak what is already in place, right?

So go now, start building your list and emailing them!

You will make mistakes; take it as part of your learning process. Learn the lessons and move on.

Borrow from the simplicity of the strategies shared in this guide and make your list building and email marketing a meaningful part of subscribers' experience with you and your brand.

The one thing that I love most about email marketing is that it can be automated; thus, generating a constant flow of sales for your product and/or services.

So enough dreaming, start practicing.

I will love to hear your success story.

Best,

James.